AutoFocus

PORSCHE 911

Auto Focus

PORSCHE 911

Richard Lentinello

MetroBooks

MetroBooks

An Imprint of the Michael Friedman Publishing Group, Inc.

©2000 by Michael Friedman Publishing Group, Inc.
First MetroBooks edition 2002

Library of Congress Cataloging-in-Publication Data

Lentinello, Richard A.
    Porsche 911 / by Richard A. Lentinello
        p. cm. —
    Includes index.
    ISBN 1-58663-876-9
        1. Porsche 911 automobile. I. Title.

TL215.P75 L46 2000
629.222'2—dc21
                                        0033568

Editors: Ann Kirby-Payne and Alexandra Bonfante-Warren
Art Director: Jeff Batzli
Designer: Kevin Ullrich
Photography Editors: Erin Feller and Kathleen Wolfe
Production Manager: Maria Gonzalez

Color separations by Colourscan Overseas Co. Pte. Ltd.
Printed in China by Leefung-Asco Printers Ltd.

1 3 5 7 9 10 8 6 4 2

For bulk purchases and special sales, please contact:
Michael Friedman Publishing Group, Inc.
Attention: Sales Department
230 Fifth Avenue
New York, NY 10001
212/685-6610 FAX 212/685-3916

Visit our website:
www.metrobooks.com

4

Contents

Introduction
A Sports Car Like No Other

Fast. Powerful. Stylish. These are just three of the most alluring characteristics of what may very well be the greatest sports car ever created: the Porsche 911.

With its distinctive fastback shape purposely designed to effectively slice through the air with minimal drag, a high-performance six-cylinder engine as reliable as it is powerful, and a no-nonsense race car–like interior designed to enhance driver fulfillment to the fullest, the Porsche 911 is like no other car ever made.

With its roots dating back to the first Porsche automobile, designed and built in 1948 in the small town of Gmünd, Austria, the 911 has evolved into the ultimate expression of Prof. Ferdinand Porsche's original sports car concept. That idea was based on a design that placed the engine and gearbox behind the rear wheels, clothed with an aerodynamic fastback coupe body that provided a cozy seating environment for two. It's a highly successful concept that has garnered worldwide acclaim and an extensive record of noted competition successes since its inception more than half a century ago. And it remains the foundation of today's latest 911 iteration, the 996.

That first Porsche design was named the 356 and lasted, with several minor body and engine alterations, until 1964. Then came the 911. Although the engine/gearbox arrangement and chassis design remained basically the same as that of the 356, the

~~~
Above: **One of the most recognizable automotive symbols of all time, the Porsche shield represents quality, speed, and excitement.**

Opposite: **A half-century of lineage is represented by this side-by-side comparison of an early 356 (left) and a late 911.**

new 911 featured a six-cylinder engine that was far more powerful and tractable than the earlier model's flat-four. The exterior still retained the basic body outline and proportions of the 356, but looked far more contemporary with its less rounded styling and sharper-edged details.

The heart of any 911 is its engine. Evolved from Volkswagen's flat-four, Porsche's version features six air-cooled, horizontally opposed cylinders topped with a single overhead camshaft on each bank of cylinders. By design, it revs quickly, with a distinctive, glorious sound that only a Porsche flat-six can orchestrate. At 5,000-plus rpm, it creates some of the finest mechanical notes ever heard, and enjoyed, by human drivers.

Driving excitement is really what the 911 experience is all about. These fascinating automobiles, regardless of their year or model designation, are a blast to drive, especially while speeding along challenging twisting back roads through the countryside where the lack of traffic allows you to experience the 911's exceptional handling, and power, to the fullest. Try it once, and you'll be forever smitten—guaranteed.

Although an adrenaline rush is quickly achieved by smashing the throttles wide open, the 911's road-holding performance is equally impressive. Aside from the 1964–68 short-wheelbase models, which required a higher level of driving ability and concentration to keep them on the road while cornering at speed, the

longer-wheelbase models from 1969 on can carve through turns as if they were magnetized to the road surface. And with the engine and gearbox positioned in the rear, the lightweight front end enhances the already extraordinarily precise rack-and-pinion steering to the point of being ultracommunicative. Factor in the 911's low center of gravity, excellent power-to-weight ratio, and inspiring brakes, and it becomes nearly impossible to find a more agile road machine that can also be tossed around at will with pinpoint accuracy.

To satisfy all the different driving desires of the world's loyal Porsche enthusiasts, the 911 has been made available in four distinct body styles at various periods of its existence: the coupe, the convertible, the Speedster, and the Targa. Each version is unique in its own right, providing a similar but distinctively special driving sensation.

The 911's incredible all-around performance is directly attributable to the Porsche factory's expansive competition program, which began during the heyday of the 356. Nearly every change that has been made to the 911's chassis structure, body, engine, gearbox,

suspension, and brakes through the years can be traced to the factory's extensive research and development of racing 911s on racetracks throughout the world before those components were installed on the production cars. From tough, long-distance twenty-four-hour races like Le Mans and Daytona that really push a car's ability to the limit to equally arduous races such as the 12 Hours of Sebring and Sicily's grueling Targa Florio, the Porsche 911 has succeeded where others have failed. All told, the Porsche 911 has probably won more automobile races than any other make or model of car ever created—clearly a result of Porsche's honed-to-perfection approach to automobile design.

For the enthusiast seeking to make the dream of Porsche ownership come true, the time has never been better to get yourself behind the wheel of this truly great sports car. Because it has been in production for nearly forty years, and because just about half of all 911s produced have been sold in the United States, the supply of older models is quite plentiful, especially in California, where nearly half of those

imported into the United States were sold. The parts are easy to come by, too, with nearly all mechanical, body, trim, and interior components available through numerous aftermarket parts manufacturers. The 911 market is also backed by an unusually large supply of specialists that have gone into business to satisfy the never ending requirements of Porsche enthusiasts seeking quality maintenance, restoration, or modification services. No matter where you travel in the world, chances are there's a Porsche specialist nearby—such is the demand to keep these fascinating sports cars on the road and performing at their best.

As its fortieth birthday approaches, the Porsche 911 has gained a loyal following of thousands of fanatical enthusiasts whose lives revolve around this amazing masterpiece of engineering. In short, it's the perfect driving machine for those who love to drive. Its rare combination of cutting-edge engineering, timeless styling, extraordinary road holding, and rip-roaring acceleration is neatly wrapped in a compact package that is stone reliable and durable in the extreme. Porsche 911: nothing even comes close.

Chapter One

The 2-Liter Models
1965–1977

The 1960s was an era of power; the bohemian generation worshiped "flower power" while muscle car enthusiasts craved horsepower. Then there were the more sophisticated proponents of small European sports cars who also desired lots of horsepower, though this horsepower had to be balanced by substantial stopping power, not to mention rewarding cornering performance. To satisfy their demanding style of driving, a new sports car tailor-made entirely for them had just been released by Porsche: it was called the 911.

Building upon the success of Porsche's first sports car, the nimble little 356, the 911 enhanced everything that made the older model so good. The ride became more compliant, the steering more responsive, the handling more inspiring, the interior more ergonomic, the shape more contemporary. For the period, the 911 was the world's greatest sports car—a claim that many aficionados feel still holds true.

First introduced into the U.S. market in California in July 1965, the 911 was Porsche's first new car in seventeen years. Designed by Prof. Ferdinand Porsche, Sr's grandson, Ferdinand, who went by the nickname "Butzi," the handsome little fastback coupe took the sports car world by storm. Weighing in at a svelte 2,376 pounds (1,079kg), its 1,991cc flat-six air-cooled aluminum engine produced 148 horsepower at 6,100

Opposite: In 1974, laughing at the world's fear of a dwindling oil supply, Porsche released the most terrifying sports car to date, the 930 Turbo. With its muscular, wide body and 3.0-liter flat-six, it produced 260 hp and a remarkable 343 lbs.-ft. of tire-scorching torque.

Above: Introduced at the the Frankfurt Auto Show in 1965, the Targa—with its steel roll bar—was billed as "the world's first safety convertible."

rpm, allowing it to reach 60 mph (96kph) from a standing start in only 8 seconds and a top speed of 130 mph (209kph). Very impressive.

Like the 356 before it, the 911 was of unit body construction and had a rear drive layout. With its engine located behind the centerline of the rear wheels, the transaxle positioned just ahead between the rear wheels, and the driver up front, it had a weight bias toward the rear that made handling a little tricky for those unfamiliar with such a layout. But the design worked, and worked well.

The early 911s—1965 to 1968—are known as the short-wheelbase models because they had the shortest wheelbase of any 911 produced. This made their handling characteristics the most sensitive of the entire 911 series. Nonetheless, the early 911s are loaded with charm. They're fun to drive and easy to maintain, making them a sports car enthusiast's delight.

For those on a budget, Porsche introduced the 912 in 1966. Nearly identical to the 911, including the same body, brakes, and suspension, it was powered by a 102-hp flat-four engine instead of a six. Still, it was able to reach a top speed of around 115 mph (185kph).

The first high-performance version appeared in 1967, and was labeled the 911S. With a tweaked engine and a pair of triple-barrel Weber carburetors, it produced a remarkable 180 hp. It had a top speed of 140 mph (225kph) and could go from 0 to 60 mph (96kph) in just 6.5 seconds.

In 1968, Porsche gave in to U.S. demand for an automatic and introduced a semi-automatic transmission called the Sportomatic. Although it robbed the 911 of power, it made driving through traffic effortless. Porsche also introduced the Targa, with its removable roof panel.

The first major change in the 911's production came in 1969, when the wheelbase was lengthened 2.2 inches (5.5cm), making its handling far more neutral. Weighing only 2,249 pounds (1,021kg), this was the lightest 911 ever built. The 911T and 911E were also introduced in 1969. The T was the base model, while the E was the next model up. The 190-hp S was still king, though, especially with its new mechanical fuel injection.

Larger 2.2-liter engines were installed in the 1970–71 models, followed by 2.4-liter engines for the 1972–73 cars. Then came the 2.7-liter engines in 1974, along with Bosch's new electronic fuel injection, K-Jetronic. To commemorate twenty-five years of production, a special Diamond Silver Metallic 911 was offered in 1975. With only 750 built, each is highly prized.

After a five-year absence, the 912 returned in 1976 with the 86-hp 2.0-liter engine from the 914. And with the new 924 just released, Porsche offered only one 911 model in 1977: a 157-hp 2.7 available in either coupe or Targa form.

Right: The 1973 Targa is a great all-around sports car, offering both closed- and open-top motoring, Bosch mechanical fuel injection for greater performance and drivability, and clean, early-911 styling.

Left: Early 911s such as this 1960s example exhibit a purity of styling that was lost on the 1974-on cars with their larger bumpers.

Above: The block-lettered 911 nameplate first appeared on the 1967 models. Earlier models sported the 911 designation on an angle.

Left: A big four-spoke steering wheel allows for good visibility of the vast instrument panel.

Opposite: The 911 was an evolving design, as evidenced by the lines of this early 1960s 356 twin-grille coupe.

Above: The Targa Florio was named for the famous road race around the coastline of Sicily, and the polished stainless steel covering the integrated roll hoop was the Targa's identifying mark. In the mid-1970s, Porsche designers changed the hoop to matte black.

Right: The most popular wheel ever to grace a 911 was the distinctive Fuchs forged-alloy. Introduced on the 1967 S, these handsome five-spokes were 5 pounds, 1 1/2 ounces (2.3 kg) lighter than standard steel wheels. Originally 14 inches (35.6 cm) in diameter, later Fuchses grew to 15 inches (38.1 cm).

Opposite: **This 1965 dashboard is classic early 911, with its wood veneer, black-faced gauges with light green markings and chrome bezels, and a wood-rimmed steering wheel with four black inner spokes.**

Above: **One of the greatest 911 models ever created was the 1967 S. Free of power-robbing emission controls, it sported a pair of triple-barrel downdraft Weber carburetors and an aggressive camshaft that helped it reach a wild 160 hp, all of which made this short-wheelbase car very entertaining to drive.**

Above: **A thin bumper is nicely integrated with the clean front-end styling. Its light weight made steering more responsive than later models.**

Right: **Early 911s, like this suavely elegant 1965 model, sported slab-sided bodywork with minimum flaring around the wheelwells and 911 script lettering on the right side of the trunk.**

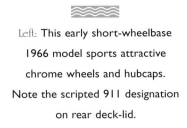

Left: This early short-wheelbase 1966 model sports attractive chrome wheels and hubcaps. Note the scripted 911 designation on rear deck-lid.

Right: The early models had finely crafted horn grilles mounted with four screws and made of chrome-plated brass, as seen on this 1965 911. In 1967, the grilles were replaced with less expensive ones, which required only two screws to mount. The driving lamps were optional.

The 3-Liter Models
1978-1998

As it entered its fifteenth year of production since being introduced to the European market back in 1964, like a youthful teenager, the 911 gracefully developed with each passing year until it matured into the outstanding road car that it is today. Unlike the lighter, smaller-displacement versions of the early 1970s, the 3-liter-powered models put on considerable weight because of the addition of supplementary accessories, enhanced creature comforts, and required safety features, all of which transformed the 911 into more of a grand touring car than a raw, all-out sports car.

Acclaimed by journalists everywhere as being one of the best GT cars in the world, the new 1978 911 SC was powered by an updated version of the old 2.7-liter flat-six, albeit with a few special modifications. It featured a stiffer aluminum crankcase in lieu of the cast-magnesium cases used from 1968 to 1977 and a redesigned crankshaft that was much stronger than previous versions. Because it was encased in larger bearing shells, the engine's bottom end was now virtually indestructible. Engine displacement was enlarged by increasing the bore diameter by 5 millimeters, thus making the normally aspirated 3.0-liter engine more tractable and enduring than any Porsche engine before. It was also substantially more powerful, developing 172 hp in U.S. trim (8 hp less than the European version), and had a torque curve

Opposite: **Custom touches like aftermarket wheels are a popular 911 modification, even on limited production models like this 1998 Cabriolet.**
Above: **The Targa nameplate evokes images of racing flat-out on winding roads through Sicilian towns, the roof open to the skies above.**

that was higher and flatter, which made the 911 driving experience considerably more pleasant. Desirable options included the rear whale-tail spoiler to enhance high-speed stability and larger, 16-inch (40.5cm) wheels that sharpened steering response and increased cornering performance. Top speed was slightly more than 130 mph (209kph), while 0–60 mph (96kph) times dropped to about 6.6 seconds.

The 1979 911 was basically the same as the 1978 model, apart from a redesigned clutch and serv assisted brakes that were now standard. This was als the year that the undesirable Sportomatic transmissio was withdrawn from production.

As the average 911 buyer got progressively older, the demand for added comfort grew. Porsche responded by offering leather-upholstered seats and headlamp washers as standard features starting in 1980. Until now, the 911 was available in either a coupe or Targa body style, but to broaden the 911's appeal, the first-ever convertible version was added to the 1983 model lineup. The public was highly receptive to this extroverted mode of fast transportation, regardless of its steep $4,500 surcharge over the coupe's $29,950 base price. And like all 1978–83 models, power remained the same at 172 hp. The year 1983 also saw the last use of the SC nomenclature. From here on in, all 911s would be known as Carreras.

Left: When, in October of 1982, Porsche introduced the 1983 911SC Cabriolet in Germany, it was the only Porsche convertible at the time. Its 3.0-liter engine displaced 2,993cc and developed 180 hp at 5,500 rpm in U.S. trim.

Right: Added to meet Department of Transportation standards in the United States, the "third light" on this Speedster model makes it look like a cyclops.

Pages 30–31: Porsche's flat-six engine has proven extremely durable and powerful, which is why 911s have been successfully raced throughout the world at both the club and professional levels. From Le Mans to Sebring, 911s have won more races than any other sports car.

Left: Drivers are guaranteed top-down, high-speed fun in the sun when piloting late-model 911s like this 1989 Carrera Cabriolet.

Opposite: This 1989 Speedster has been substantially modified with a deep front air dam that flows into extended fender flares. Driving lights, an oil cooler, and a six-point roll bar add to the racy look.

Left: Its design based on the original, this 1993 993 is the last of the true 911s.

Right: With its shape nearly identical to the coupe's roofline, the snug-fitting two-layer canvas convertible top is very effective at keeping the elements at bay.

Pages 36–37: The ultimate turbo-charged racer will always be the 959. This 1998 S model shows off more than 500 hp.

Left: Apart from its eye-catching
yellow coachwork, this very
special 1996 model features a
glass panel roof that slides
completely open.

Above: Power for this 1996 model
comes from a silky-smooth,
high-revving 3.6-liter flat-six that
develops a boisterous 285 hp
at 6,100 rpm.

40

Above: With its canvas in place, the cozy 1994 Speedster looks like a chopped-top Porsche street rod.

Opposite: For something completely different, this 1994 electric blue Strosek Speedster is just the ticket, with its smooth, wide body, custom headlamps, and large modular wheels.

Left: With its purposely sloped back and bulging rear fenders, the 911's no-nonsense shape reeks of heavy muscle.

Opposite: In stock form, the U.S.-spec Cabriolet for 1988 had a 3.2-liter, 217-hp engine. Only 2,116 were produced.

Left: This 1989 Speedster was
Porsche's contemporary
interpretation of the original 356
from 1955.

Fast Flyers
The Carrera Models

The 2.7-liter Carrera RS can arguably be called the greatest 911 of all time. Created so that the RSH version could be homologated for racing, Porsche enthusiasts the world over consider the RS—with its powerful free-revving 210-hp engine, nimble lightweight chassis, and no-frills, in-your-face attitude—to be the ultimate 911. And it's very, very quick, posting 0–60 mph (96kph) times around 6 seconds flat and a very impressive top speed for its time of around 152 mph (245kph). And with production limited to a scant 1,590 examples of all four versions—the RS Touring, RS Sport, RSR, and RSH—every one is highly coveted by collectors around the world.

To complement its aggressive, raging attitude both on the street and on the racetrack, the Carrera RS was fitted with a deep color-matched front air dam under its bumper, a stubby rear spoiler that affectionately became known as the duck tail, and a bold stripe just above its rocker panel with the word "Carrera" cut out in script. Most RSs were finished in white, offset by colorful stripes of blue, red, or green. With color-coded wheels to match the stripe, the RS was very racy, both in appearance and performance.

In 1974, a mass-produced Carrera for the everyday driver was made available that used the 167-hp 911S engine. Available in both coupe and Targa body styles, it featured K-Jetronic, Bosch's new electronic fuel injection system. Like the RS, it came with the

Opposite: **Color-coded bumpers and full-faced alloy wheels gave the later Carrera models a more contemporary appearance than earlier models.**
Above: **Be it on the wheel center caps or on the aluminum brake calipers behind, the name PORSCHE is proudly displayed for all to see.**

duck-tail spoiler, air dam, and scripted lettering on the sides. Meanwhile, the first U.S.-legal RS version was further upgraded with forged aluminum trailing arms, lightweight seats with high backs, an electronic tachometer, a special steering wheel, and a boost in power to 220 hp. By contrast, the ultrarare RSR racer had a mighty 320 hp.

The only two 911s offered in 1975 were the S and the whale-tail-spoilered Carrera, both with only 157 hp. Then in 1976 and 1977, the only "911" to wear the Carrera nameplate was the 930 Turbo Carrera.

It wasn't until 1984 that the desirable Carrera name reappeared. In coupe, Targa, or Cabriolet form, it now sported a 3.2-liter engine fitted with the newly developed Motronic control system, which helped make the 200-hp engine far more efficient. Added features were bigger brakes and a front spoiler fitted with fog lights. And for those flashy types, a "Turbo Look" package—but without the turbo—was offered. The 1984–86 models were essentially identical. For 1987 and 1988, the Carrera received a boost in power to 214 hp, a new hydraulic-type clutch, and a redesigned 5-speed gearbox, allowing it to reach a top speed of 157 mph (253kph).

To enhance its already wide appeal, the 1989 Carrera was offered in two models: a 214-hp 3.2 like the previous year's offering, and the all-new four-wheel-drive version, aptly labeled the Carrera 4, fitted with a larger 3.6 engine that developed a potent 247 hp. The Carrera 4 was fitted with antilock brakes and a rear spoiler that raised automatically above 55 mph (88kph). Further enhancements came in 1990 with standard dual front air bags and an optional 4-speed automatic transmission called Tiptronic, which provided clutchless shifting.

The Carrera 2 (a two-wheel-drive version of the Carrera 4) and 4 lived on until 1993, during which time several models and body styles were offered. These included the 260-hp Carrera 2 RS in 1991, an entry-level Carrera 2 in 1992 called the RS America, and the Carrera 2 Speedster in 1993. An all-new 911 Carrera with a smoother, more aerodynamic body appeared in 1993 under the factory designation 993, which lasted for only four years before being replaced by the all-new 996.

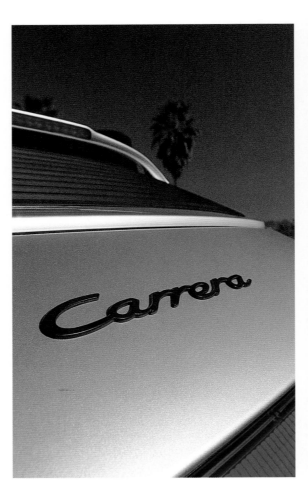

Above: The cachet of carrying the Carrera nameplate places the 911 in another league.

Right: The last iteration of the original 911 was the 993 C2 Carrera. This 1995 model features a more flowing and aerodynamic body than any previous 911.

Left: A color-matched front air dam, duck tail spoiler, and bold script above the rocker panel became the hallmarks of the Carerra RS.

Right: With its distinctive rocker panel decal and effective "duck tail" rear spoiler, the 1973 2.7-liter Carrera is truly one of the classic Porsches.

Pages 52–53: The bold graphics advertising the Carrera matched its aggressive looks. This 1975 model was the first one to come with the whale-tail spoiler.

Opposite: Although its exterior remained the same, the 3.2-liter Carrera replaced the ever-popular SC in late 1993.

Right: The 3.2-liter Carrera Cabriolet is one of the most sought-after Porsches on the used car market.

Pages 56–57: At speeds greater than 55 mph (88.5kph), the rear spoiler automatically rises to keep the rear end firmly planted to the pavement. The higher the speed, the higher the spoiler rises.

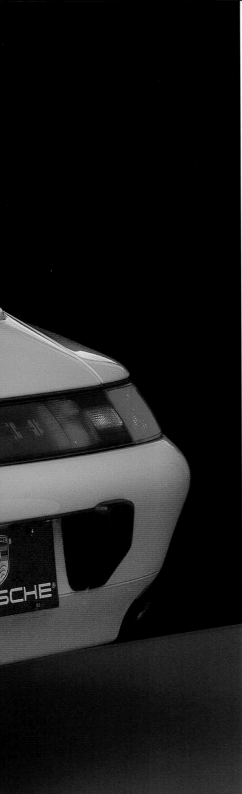

Left: In spite of the fact that it lasted only four years before it was replaced by the all-new 996, the 993 was clearly the best 911 ever built to that point.

Above: The Carrera RS had a 2.7-liter engine that delivered a stout 210-horsepower.

Left: The Carrera 2 was the two-wheel-drive version of the Carrera 4 model.

59

Left: Be it a 1965 model or a 1992 model, all 911s wear their badge proudly on their front hood.

Right: Specially designed to cool the brakes efficiently, these light-alloy five-spoke wheels are original equipment on this 1998 model.

Pages 62–63: With the 996, Porsche successfully created a cutting-edge sports car that remained squarely in the 911 tradition. Smoothly designed to slice through the air with minimal drag, the front end still has the 911 silhouette, with the hood lower than the fender tops.

Turbo Terrors
The 930

In October 1974, while automobile manufacturers were introducing powerless, fuel-efficient cars as a consequence of the previous year's oil crisis, Porsche stunned performance-starved sports car enthusiasts the world over when it introduced the quickest, most powerful 911 to date: the 930 Turbo. In short, the car was an animal; it possessed the ability to spin its rear tires into a thick cloud of smoking rubber with the least bit of throttle provocation.

The cause of all this road-burning 154-mph (248kph) -plus excitement was the result of Porsche stretching its already highly effective 2.7-liter flat-six engine to a full 3 liters and attaching a single exhaust-driven KKK turbocharger. To ensure that the specially designed forged aluminum pistons would survive the intense heat generated by the quickly spinning 80,000-plus rpm turbo, oil squirters were positioned within the stronger crankcase to keep all six pistons as cool as possible. And in the aftermath of the turbo forcing huge volumes of air into the combustion chambers, thus creating greater internal cylinder pressure, the compression had to be lowered to 6.5:1 from 8.5:1. With fuel supplied by the K-Jetronic fuel injection system, the net result was a whopping 245 hp at 5,500 rpm for U.S.-spec 930s and 260 hp for the European version.

In addition to its powerful engine and massaged drivetrain, the 1975 930 Turbo was also known for

Opposite: This 930 Turbo features the popular period modification of BBS three-piece modular wheels.

Above: A single KKK turbocharger transformed the 911 from a fast sports cars into a 154-mph (248kph) road rocket.

its tough appearance. To set this very special 911 apart from its more sedate siblings, the 930's most distinguishing characteristics were a deep front air dam, a large whale-tail rear spoiler, and very wide flared fenders. This combination of tough, racy looks backed by serious muscle was magical, replacing the red Ferrari as every young boy's exotic dream machine.

As the 930 aged, it went through a series of evolutionary changes, not the least of which was a sizable increase in horsepower in its later years. Benefiting from the 911's new rust-resistant zinc-coated body shell, the 1976 and 1977 Turbos were basically unchanged apart from a slightly larger rear spoiler and the addition of electronically adjusted door mirrors. The big change came in 1978 when the engine's displacement was increased to 3.3 liters. To handle the 265 hp (300 hp in European trim), larger cross-drilled ventilated brake rotors and four-piston calipers from the 917 race car were fitted, which dramatically improved stopping ability. Then, in 1979, sales of the 930 in the United States were temporarily halted.

A more powerful 930 Turbo that sported 282 hp at 5,500 rpm returned to the United States in 1986. Then, in 1987, the 930S appeared with optional Slant-Nose body panels featuring pop-up headlights and large air scoops ahead of the rear wheels, making it the most radical-looking Turbo of all. And, for the first time, in 1988 Porsche offered the Turbo in Targa and Cabriolet form in addition to the coupe.

Starting in 1991, the latest iteration of the Turbo became known as the 964T. Fitted with a larger turbo and intercooler, it made 320 hp at 5,750 rpm. Then, in 1993, a displacement increase to 3.6 liters produced an incredibly potent 360-hp engine, clearly making this 964T the greatest Turbo terror of them all.

Right: This excellent example of an all-original Turbo coupe is one of only 1,424 930s sold in the U.S. in 1986, after a six-year absence from the market.

Left: Many 930 slantnose front fenders feature seven louvers to help draw heat away from the brakes.

Opposite: This 1979 935 was a gift from Porsche to R.D. Whittington, Jr., for winning Le Mans. It is specially painted in the Whittington team colors.

Pages 70–71: Koenig, a noted German customizer, built several of these radically modified Turbo convertibles. This 1985 model looks very sinister in black.

Left: The 1997 Turbo has 400 hp and a new six-speed gearbox.

Right: The ultimate Turbo for Porsche power fanatics: a sleek, late-1980s slantnose convertible.

Left: With its vast power-to-weight ratio, the 1997 Turbo comes close to the speedometer-indicated top speed of 200 mph (321.8kph).

Above: Later models featured a very wide whale tail spoiler and "twisted" five-spoke alloy wheels to aid brake cooling.

Opposite: Aftermarket body panels such as this front air dam and rocker panel covers were used extensively by customizers in the 1980s.

Below: To keep the turbo spinning in its power band, designers gave it six forward close-ratio gears.

Right: Black wheels with polished rims were characteristic features of the early 930s.

Left: Specially designed air scoops direct air to keep rear brakes cool.

Below: Color-matched interiors were popularized by European customizers.

Opposite: Modeled after Porsche's successful 936 race cars, slant-nose front ends eventually made their way into production 911's.

Above: The 1988 959 features
a rounded, flowing body shape
that envelops the entire exterior,
as demonstrated by this front
fender, which streams into the
rocker panel.

Right: The Cabriolet 930 was
introduced in 1988 alongside the
Targa and Coupe versions.

Left: The huge rear whale tail spoiler was necessary to keep the rear end firmly planted on the road surface at high speeds.

Above: Below the blacked-out grille resides an air-to-air intercooler that connects to the engine's intake manifold.

Pages 84–85: Brumos Porsche, a Jacksonville, Florida, Porsche dealer, sponsored many championship-winning Porsches, including this highly competitive 500-plus-hp 935.

Chapter Five

The Next Gener

The 996

Finally, after more than thirty-three years with essentially the same body and chassis structure, engine, and suspension design, the evolution of the 911 suddenly turned revolutionary with the introduction of the 996 body style in 1999. Although the entire car was designed and engineered from a clean sheet of paper, Porsche successfully retained the 911's original look. The new 911 has improved ergonomics that have made the cabin roomier and more comfortable than any previous model.

Always the heart of a 911, the engine is all new, too. Retaining its flat-six heritage and rear-mounted position, it features a conventional water-cooled block and cylinder heads for the first time. Displacing 3387cc, it's an oversquare design with a 3.77-inch (9.5cm) bore and 3.07-inch (8cm) stroke. Built entirely of aluminum, it's a twin-cam design with two camshafts per cylinder head operating four valves per cylinder for maximum breathing ability. With an 11.3:1 compression ratio, it puts out a remarkable 296 hp at 6,800 rpm, allowing it to hit a top speed of 174 mph (280kph); 0–60 mph (96kph) takes only 5 seconds. A 6-speed manual gearbox or 5-speed Tiptronic semi-automatic are the two transmission choices.

To ensure positive stopping, huge 12.5-inch (32cm) vented rotors reside up front with nearly as large 11.8-inch (30cm) discs in the rear, both of which

Opposite: The 1999 996 thrusts the 911 concept into the twenty-first century with a new chassis, engine, and suspension. A completely restyled body retains the 911's distinctive silhouette. Above: When the car reaches a speed of 75 mph (120.7kph), the rear spoiler automatically begins to elevate in order to keep the rear end firmly planted.

"ultimate" can be applied to a car, this 911 Turbo clearly deserves it.

Having entered its third yeard of production, in 2001 the 996's styling tweaks were made to give it more of a distinctive appearance than the lower-priced entry-level Boxster, which made its debut in 1997. These changes include a squarer-looking front end, wider rear fenders, and composite headlight clusters from the higher-priced Turbo model. And the engine has been improved as well, with a displacement increase of 200cc, which delivers a moderate power increase.

As one expects of Porsche, no matter how incredibly refined and near-perfect its new 911 may be, there's already an all-new replacement scheduled for the year 2003, thus guaranteeing future generations the joys of 911 ownership.

Left: Although its aesthetics are very contemporary, the unmistakable fastback profile still proclaims that it's a 911.

Above: The layered instrument panel of the 996 gives the illusion of three dimensions. The front and center tachometer reminds drivers of the car's real purpose.

Right: The invitingly sleek shape casts a spell upon all those who enter its form-fitting cabin, making this an ideal way to add points to one's license.

Pages 92–93: The 996's new body and chassis are complemented by a re-engineered flat-six engine that, for the first time in 911 history, is water-cooled. Displacing 3.4 liters, this all-aluminum gem produces a healthy 296 hp at 6,800 rpm and 258 lb.-ft. of torque at 4,600 rpm. Up top, the double overhead cams and four-valve-per-cylinder heads are fed by electronic sequential-port fuel injection. Meanwhile, behind those handsome, cast-alloy, eighteen-inch (45.7cm), five-spoke wheels reside ventilated cross-drilled discs with huge Brembo billet-aluminum, four-piston calipers for maximum braking performance. Owners may choose their gearboxes: either a Getrag-built manual six-speed or a five-speed ZF Tiptronic automatic.

Right: Wind-tunnel-tested to achieve an optimal drag coefficient of 0.30, every square inch of the 996's smooth exterior has been meticulously designed to minimize aerodynamic drag at speed.

Suggested Reading

Adler, Dennis. *Porsche 911 Road Cars.* Osceola, Wisconsin: Motorbooks International, 1998.

Batchelor, Dean, and Randy Leffingwell. *Illustrated Porsche Buyer's Guide.* Osceola, Wisconsin: Motorbooks International, 1997.

Cotton, Michael. *Porsche 911 and Derivatives: A Collector's Guide: From 1981.* Osceola, Wisconsin: Motorbooks International, 1994.

Cutler, Robert, and Bob Fendell. *The Encyclopedia of Automobile Racing Greats.* New Jersey: Prentice Hall, 1973.

Frere, Paul. *Porsche 911 Story.* Haynes Publications, 1997.

Jensinson, Denis. *Porsche 356: Coupe, Cabriolet, Roadster, Speedster & Carrera.* United Kingdom: Osprey Publications, 1999.

Miller, Susann. *Porsche: Power, Performance, and Perfection.* New York: Michael Friedman Publishing Group, 1996.

Morgan, Peter. *Original Porsche 911.* Osceola, Wisconsin: Motorbooks International, 1998.

Orgeson, Griffith, and Eugene Jaderquist. *Sports and Classic Cars.* Englewood Cliffs, New Jersey: Prentice Hall, 1955.

Spiro, Don. *Roadsters: Fifty Years of Top-Down Speed.* New York: Michael Friedman Publishing Group, 2000.

Wagner, Rob L. *Classic Cars.* New York: Michael Friedman Publishing Group, 1996.

Wagner, Rob Leicester. *Style & Speed: The World's Greatest Sports Cars.* New York: Michael Friedman Publishing Group, 1998.

Index

Photography Credits

Automobile Quarterly Publications: pp. 28–29, 34–35

©Neill Bruce: pp. 12–13, 18 left, 18–19, 32, 38–39, 39 right, 59 bottom, 78 right, 79, 80 left

©Corbis: pp. 4–5, 76

©Ron Kimball: pp. 6–7, 8, 26, 30–31, 33, 34 left, 36–37, 41, 43, 44–45, 48–49, 52–53, 54, 56–57, 58–59, 60–61, 62–63, 65, 66–67, 68, 70–71, 72–73, 80–81, 82–83, 84–85, 87, 88–89, 92–93

©David B. Lyons: pp. 40, 69

©Dom Miliano: pp. 9, 11, 14–15, 15 right, 16, 29 right, 51, 59 top

©David Newhardt: pp. 17, 20, 22 left, 22–23, 25 right, 27, 47, 48 left, 60 left, 72 left, 74–75, 77 left, 86, 89 right

©Roy B. Query: pp. 21, 24–25, 55, 64, 77 right

©Leonard Turner: pp. 10, 46, 50, 75 right, 78 left, 90 left

©Zoomstock: pp. 2, 42, 83 right, 90–91